Are You a Forever Family?

**Words By
Marcy Bursac**

Pictures By
Mallory Cheatham

To children in the United States who are waiting to be adopted.

To request bulk copies of this book, contact distribution@bookbaby.com.
Paperback ISBN: 978-1-66784-072-7
Ebook ISBN: 978-1-66784-073-4
First paperback edition May 2022 – National Foster Care Month.

Printed in the USA.
BookBaby
7905 Crescent Blvd.
Pennsauken, NJ 08110
www.BookBaby.com

Some children need a forever family.

Some forever families adopt one child.

Some forever families adopt a group of children.

Sometimes people in a forever family look alike.

Sometimes people in a forever family don't look alike.

A forever family lives together.

A forever family takes care of their children.

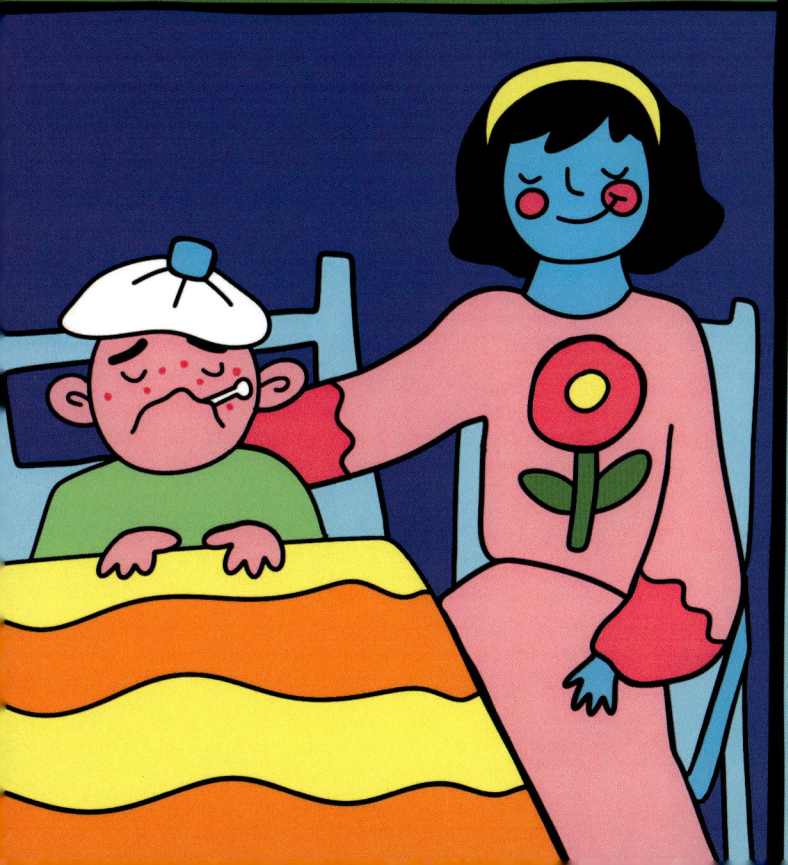

In the United States, there are
115,000

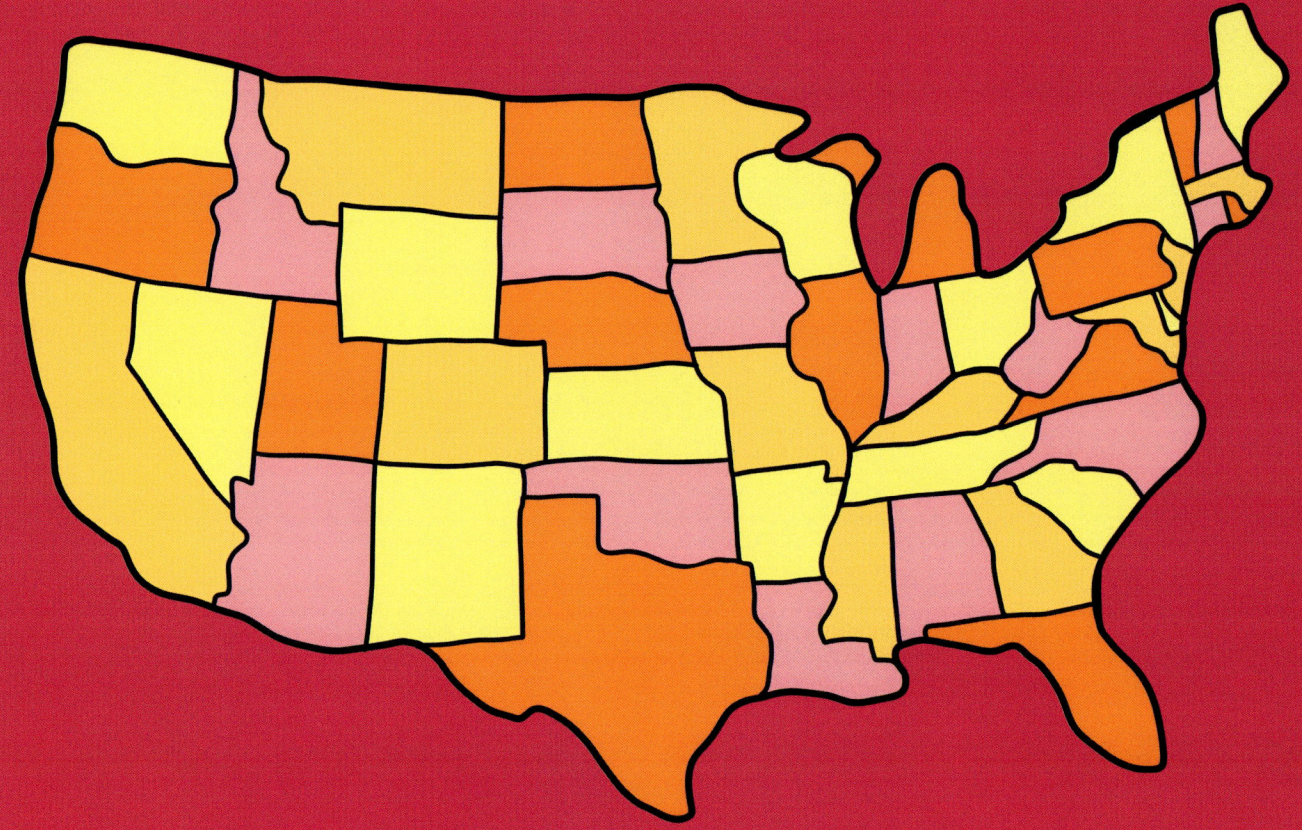

children who are waiting for their forever family.

They are waiting because we need more families to adopt children and sibling groups in the United States.

Who Can be A Forever Family?

Anne is an adult but she is not married.

She became a forever family.

Ben and Emily are unable to have biological children.

They became a forever family.

Joe and Jane have adult children.
They became a forever family.

Alice is a single parent.

She became a forever family.

Rob and Reece are married but do not have children.

They became a forever family.

Nancy has grandkids.

She became a forever family.

Nathan and Marcy have no children but want to adopt. They became a forever family.

Some people want to adopt but think it costs a lot of money.

Adopting a child waiting in the United States costs

You could be A Forever Family.

Are you a forever family?

Also by Marcy Bursac:

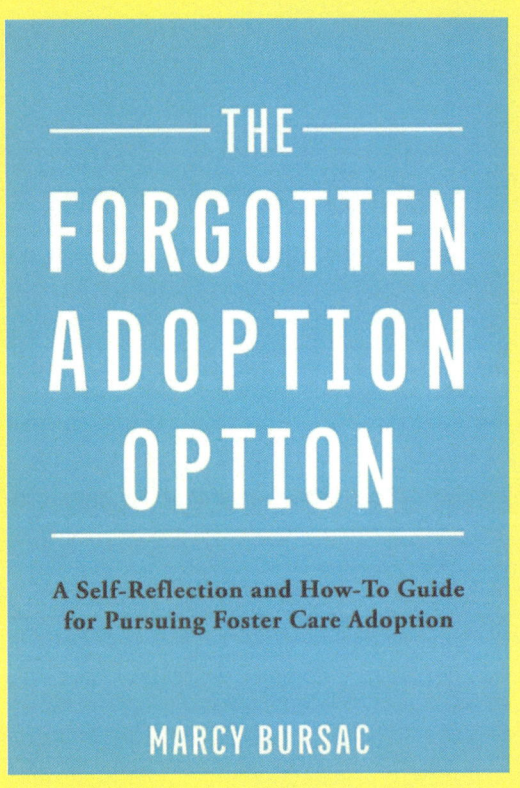

Foster care adoption was Marcy's Plan A.
She and her husband adopted a biological sibling pair.

While remote schooling her children during the pandemic, Marcy began to see a gap between adults with a desire to adopt and the 115,000 adoptable children within the United States.